W9-AWQ-221

THE HISTORY OF THE DALLAS COWBOYS

Published by Creative Education
123 South Broad Street
Mankato, Minnesota 56001
Creative Education is an imprint of The Creative Company.

DESIGN AND PRODUCTION BY **EVANSDAY DESIGN**

Copyright © 2005 Creative Education.
International copyright reserved in all countries.
No part of this book may be reproduced in any form
without written permission from the publisher.
Printed in the United States of America

LIBRARY OF CONGRESS CATALOGING-IN-PUBLICATION DATA

Hawkes, Brian (Brian F.)
The history of the Dallas Cowboys / by Brian Hawkes.
p. cm. — (NFL today)
Summary: Traces the history of the team from its beginnings through 2003.
ISBN 978-1-58341-294-7
1. Dallas Cowboys (Football team)—History—Juvenile literature. [1. Dallas
Cowboys (Football team)—History. 2. Football—History.] I. Title. II. Series.

GV956.D3H39 2004
796.332'64'0976442812—dc22   2003065111

9 8

COVER PHOTO: safety Roy Williams

796.332
HAW

RISING FROM THE ENDLESS STRETCHES OF TEXAS PRAIRIE IS THE CITY OF DALLAS. THE SECOND-LARGEST CITY IN TEXAS, DALLAS LIES ALONG THE TRINITY RIVER IN THE NORTHERN PART OF THE STATE. IT WAS NAMED AFTER GEORGE MIFFLIN DALLAS, WHO WAS THE VICE PRESIDENT OF THE UNITED STATES WHEN THE CITY WAS FOUNDED IN 1846. TODAY, DALLAS IS THE LEADING BANKING AND FINANCIAL HUB OF THE SOUTHWEST, AS WELL AS A MAJOR CENTER FOR PUBLISHING, ADVERTISING, AND MANUFACTURING. DALLAS IS IN THE HEART OF FOOTBALL COUNTRY. HIGH SCHOOL FOOTBALL IS A CELEBRATED TRADITION IN TEXAS, AND POWERHOUSE COLLEGE FOOTBALL TEAMS SUCH AS THE UNIVERSITY OF TEXAS, TEXAS TECH, AND TEXAS A&M BATTLE FOR STATE SUPREMACY. BUT SINCE 1959, RESIDENTS OF THE "LONE STAR" STATE HAVE PERHAPS CHEERED MOST PASSIONATELY FOR THE PROFESSIONAL TEAM WITH THE LONE STAR ON ITS HELMET—THE NATIONAL FOOTBALL LEAGUE'S (NFL) DALLAS COWBOYS.

[Running back Herschel Walker]

THE NFL FIRST came to Texas in 1952. The Dallas Texans, as that first team was called, had high hopes but won only one game in its first season. Worse yet, few people were interested in watching the team play. At the end of that first season, the Texans dropped out of the league.

By 1959, the NFL was looking to expand again. Dallas multimillionaire Clint Murchison Jr. was excited by the idea of bringing pro football back to his hometown. He hired Tex Schramm, the former general manager of the Los Angeles Rams, to help put together a winning franchise. To make sure that the team wouldn't be confused with the franchise that had failed in 1952, Schramm came up with a new team name: the Dallas Cowboys.

Nicknamed "Dandy Don," tough quarterback Don Meredith led the Cowboys throughout the 1960s.

Since the team had not yet been formally admitted to the NFL, the Cowboys weren't allowed to participate in the league's draft in 1959. Undeterred, Schramm set his sights on acquiring the team's top priority: a quality quarterback. His first choice was a two-time All-American from local Southern Methodist University named "Dandy" Don Meredith.

To sign Meredith, Schramm asked his old friend George Halas for help. Halas, the owner of the Chicago Bears, drafted Meredith for the Bears, then traded him to the Cowboys. Schramm was also able to sign running back Don Perkins with some more behind-the-scenes help. In December 1959, Schramm named former New York Giants assistant Tom Landry the team's head coach. Finally, in early 1960, the Dallas Cowboys were officially admitted to the NFL.

Veteran quarterback Eddie LeBaron was brought in to start while Meredith adjusted to the pro game. LeBaron and the first-year Cowboys finished a woeful 0–11–1. In 1961, the Cowboys excited their fans by starting out 3–1. Unfortunately, they won only one more game the rest of the season. Still, Coach Landry saw promise in his players' work ethic. "This team has always played for me," he said.

WITH PERKINS AND MEREDITH poised to lead the Cowboys offense for years to come, Dallas chose a fast and powerful pass rusher named Bob Lilly with its first-ever draft choice in 1961. Nicknamed "Mr. Cowboy," Lilly would go on to become one of the greatest defensive tackles in NFL history, playing in 11 Pro Bowls and becoming the first Cowboys player to be inducted into the Pro Football Hall of Fame. "A player like Bob Lilly comes along just about once in a lifetime," said Coach Landry.

Even with the individual talents of Meredith, Perkins, and Lilly, the Cowboys posted losing records from 1962 to 1964. But the team continued adding defensive talent, drafting linebacker Lee Roy Jordan in 1963 and ball-hawking safety Mel Renfro in 1964. The Cowboys also boosted their offense by adding wide receiver "Bullet" Bob Hayes, a world-class sprinter, in 1965. That year, Dallas went 7–7 and made the playoffs for the first time.

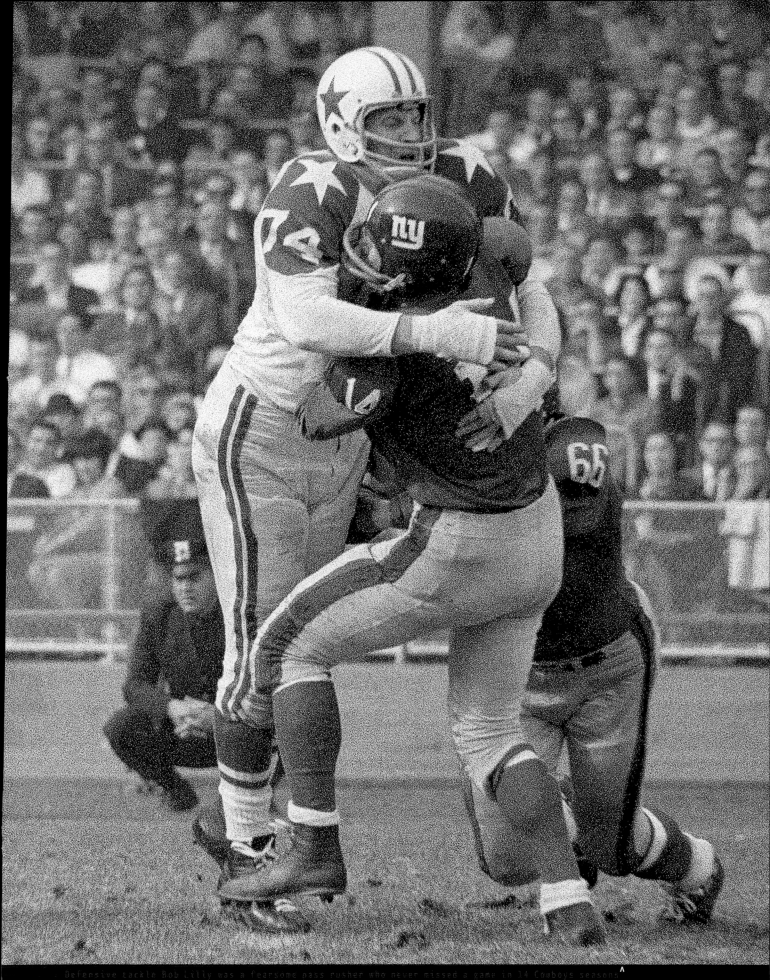

A knack for producing come-from-behind victories earned Roger the Sports Illustrated "Comeback" moniker.

Over the next four seasons, the Cowboys rode high, posting a combined 42–12–2 record. In 1966 and 1967, the young team in silver and blue charged all the way to the NFL championship game, losing to the Green Bay Packers both times. The 1967 game was a classic contest played in Green Bay in such frigid conditions that it is today remembered as the "Ice Bowl." In that game, legendary Green Bay quarterback Bart Starr scored on a late quarterback sneak to hand Dallas a bitter 21–17 defeat.

The Cowboys needed a spark to put them over the top. That spark came in the form of quarterback Roger Staubach. Staubach had played college football for the U.S. Naval Academy, and in 1963, he won the Heisman Trophy as the best college player in America. The young quarterback was drafted by the Cowboys in 1964, but before he could play pro football, he had to fulfill a four-year commitment with the Navy. When Staubach finally joined the Cowboys in 1969, the good times were about to begin in Dallas.

NICKNAMED "ROGER THE DODGER" for his scrambling abilities, Staubach immediately began winning both games and fans. During his rookie year, the Cowboys posted an 11–2–1 record. In his second season, Dallas charged all the way to the Super Bowl. Although the Cowboys suffered a painful 16–13 loss to the Baltimore Colts in that game, they came roaring right back to the Super Bowl in 1971.

This time, behind the great play of Staubach, running back Duane Thomas, and wide receivers Lance Alworth and Bob Hayes, Dallas dominated the Miami Dolphins 24–3 to win its first NFL championship. "My most satisfying moment as a professional was in that locker room in New Orleans," Staubach later said. "Dallas had been a winning team but until that moment had the reputation

Longtime defensive end Harvey Martin set a team record with 114 career quarterback sacks.

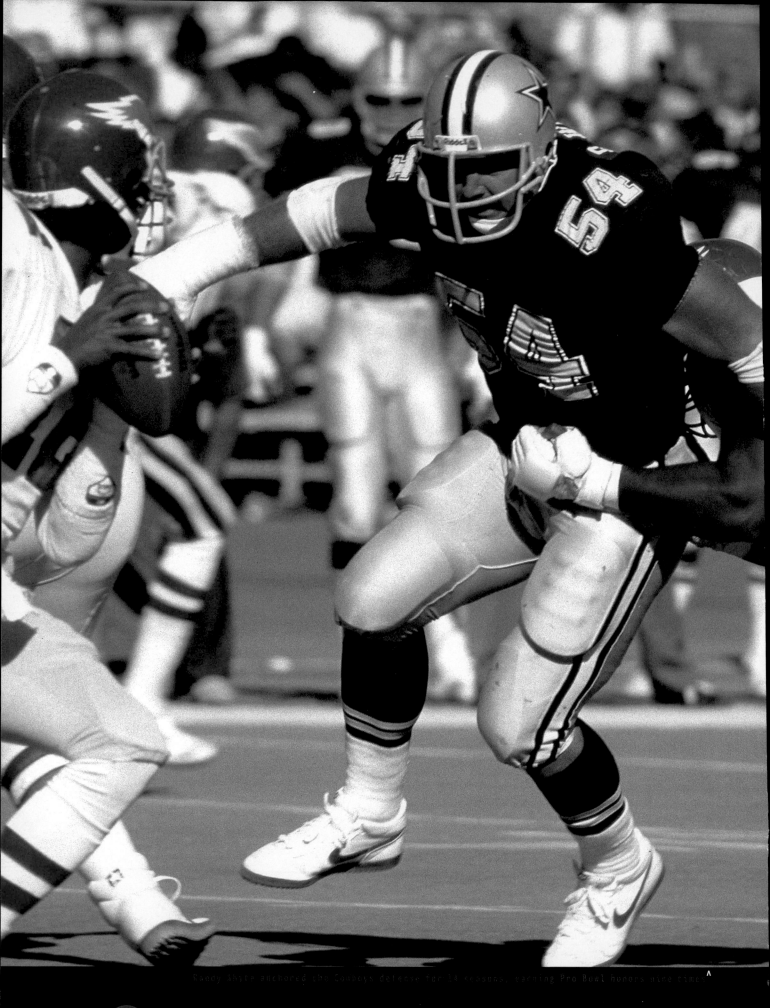

Randy White anchored the Cowboys defense for 14 seasons, earning Pro Bowl honors nine times.

of not being able to win the big one. I looked around that locker room at Bob Lilly, [linebacker] Chuck Howley, and the other veterans. I could see the pride on their faces. It was a great feeling."

Over the next seven seasons, Dallas played in five National Football Conference (NFC) championship games and three more Super Bowls. In 1975, the Cowboys met the Pittsburgh Steelers in the Super Bowl, losing 21–17. In 1977, the Cowboys faced off against the Denver Broncos in the Super Bowl; this time defensive linemen Harvey Martin and Randy White led them to a 27–10 victory. The Cowboys galloped back to the Super Bowl in 1978 but lost to the Steelers in a 35–31 shootout.

Overall, the Cowboys posted an NFL-best 105–39 record, played in five Super Bowls, and won two world championships during the 1970s. This success gained the Cowboys fans throughout the country, earning them the lasting nickname of "America's Team."

DORSETT DELIVERS EXCITEMENT>

IN 1977, A NEW STAR was born in Dallas: Heisman

Trophy-winning running back Tony Dorsett, who add-

ed an exciting new dimension to the Cowboys' offense.

Although Dorsett was only 5-foot-11 and 190 pounds,

he had the perfect mixture of speed and power. In just

his second NFL season, he rushed for 1,325 yards. Even

Dorsett was a bit surprised by his instant success. "I was

the skinny little kid from Aliquippa, Pennsylvania, who

wasn't supposed to make it," he said.

Over the next seven years, Dorsett rushed for more than

1,000 yards every year but one (only a players' strike in

1982 interrupted the streak). Before he ended his Dallas

career in 1987, Dorsett would become the team's all-time

leading rusher. He would also set an NFL record for the

longest run from scrimmage with a spectacular 99-yard

romp against the Minnesota Vikings in 1983.

Famous for his blazing speed, Tony Dorsett had five carries of 75 yards or longer in his career.

Down! Black 19 Set! Hut!

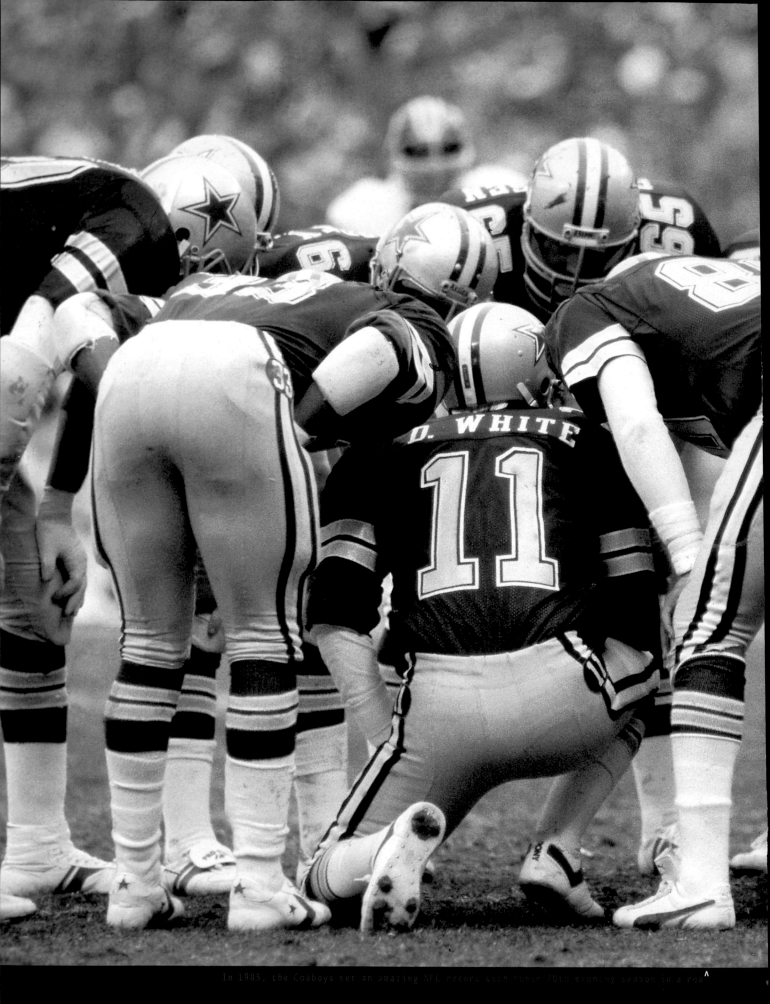

In 1983, the Cowboys set an amazing NFL record with their 20th winning season in a row. ^

In 1980, 1981, and 1982, Dorsett and the Cowboys ended their season with a loss in the NFC championship game every year. Then, in 1983, a number of Cowboys greats of the 1970s and early '80s announced their retirement. Dallas went into the 1984 season without such standouts as tight end Billy Joe Dupree and wide receiver Drew Pearson.

New Cowboys heroes soon began to step forward. Cornerback Everson Walls and powerful running back Herschel Walker turned in some exciting performances throughout the mid-1980s. But the Cowboys were no longer a powerhouse. From 1986 to 1988, they posted a losing record every year.

A NEW SHERIFF COMES TO TOWN>

ON APRIL 18, 1989, a new era in Dallas Cowboys history began when Arkansas businessman Jerry Jones bought the team. Jones was determined to turn the once-proud franchise around. One of his first moves was to replace the legendary Tom Landry—the franchise's first and only head coach—with Jimmy Johnson, the former coach of the University of Miami Hurricanes.

Coach Johnson began rebuilding the team immediately. In 1989, he made the biggest trade in NFL history, sending star running back Herschel Walker to the Minnesota Vikings for five players and six draft picks. With these draft picks, Johnson loaded the Cowboys with young talent. The Cowboys already had a rising star receiver named Michael Irvin, and with the first pick in the 1989

Speedy and sure-handed halfback Herschel Walker was Dallas's only Pro Bowl player in 1986 and 1987.

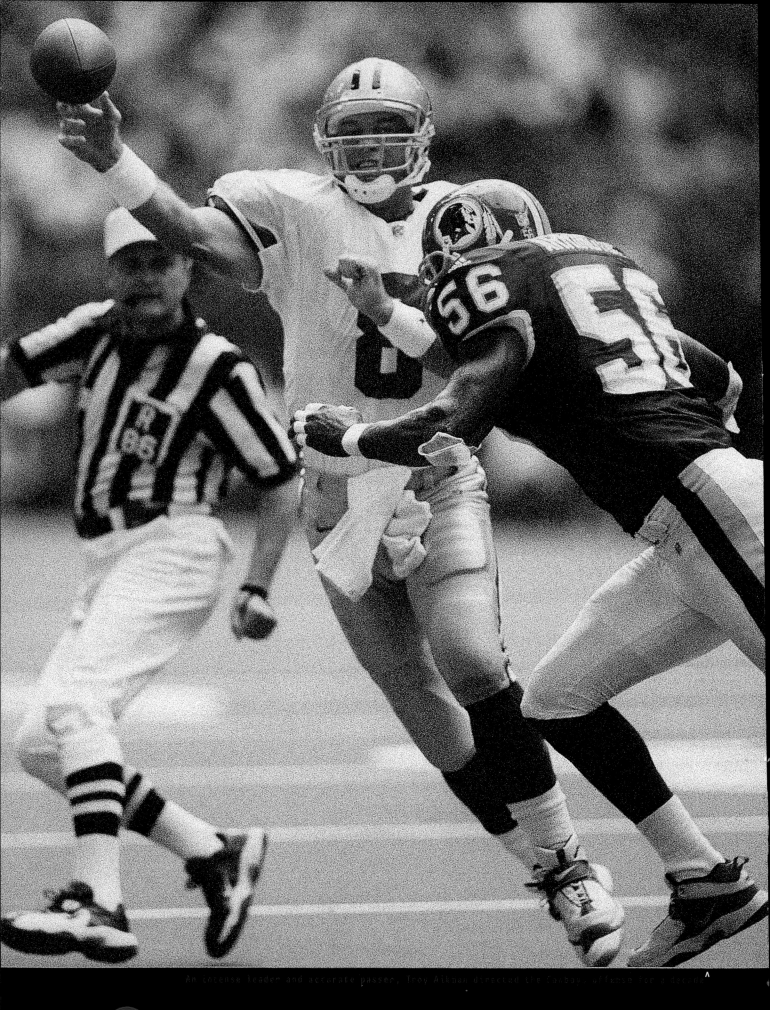

An intense leader and accurate passer, Troy Aikman directed the Cowboys offense for a decade.

Receiver Michael Irvin scored 65 career touchdowns ^

End Charles Haley was a relentless pass-rushing force ^

NFL Draft, they selected young quarterback Troy Aikman. Then, in 1990, Dallas added a short but powerful running back from the University of Florida named Emmitt Smith.

Smith was the 16th player selected in the NFL Draft, as some experts considered him too small and slow for the NFL. Smith immediately dispelled those doubts by running for 937 yards and scoring 11 touchdowns in his first NFL season—a performance that earned him NFL Offensive Rookie of the Year honors. "Sixteen teams passed on me," he said. "I was beginning to think I wouldn't go until the second round. But I hope 16 teams are kicking themselves now."

With Smith leading the ground attack and Aikman and Irvin hooking up regularly through the air, the Cowboys quickly became the scourge of the NFC once again. In 1992, Aikman threw for 3,445 yards, Smith rushed for 1,713 yards, and Irvin added 1,396 receiving yards. The defense, meanwhile, was led by fiery veteran defensive end Charles Haley. The Cowboys went 13–3 and then barreled through the playoffs to reach the Super Bowl. Aikman threw four touchdown passes and earned Super Bowl Most Valuable Player (MVP) honors as the Cowboys crushed the Buffalo Bills 52–17 to bring home their third world championship.

THE TRADITION CONTINUES>

IN 1993, THE COWBOYS returned to the Super Bowl. Smith ran wild in the big game as Dallas again trounced the Bills, this time by a 30–13 score. After falling short of the Super Bowl the next season, the Cowboys made a big move by adding Deion Sanders—an incredibly fast cornerback and kick returner nicknamed "Prime Time"—to their already deep roster.

With Sanders and the "Triplets" (Aikman, Irvin, and Smith) leading the way, the 1995 Cowboys reached the Super Bowl once again. This time they faced the Pittsburgh Steelers, the team that had twice thwarted Dallas in the Super Bowl in the 1970s. This time the Cowboys proved too powerful for the Steelers, pulling out a 27–17 victory to win their third world championship in four years.

In 1995, flashy cornerback Deion Sanders helped Dallas reach its NFL-record eighth Super Bowl.

Kennedy Library
77th and Central Ave.
Burbank, L 60459

Down! Blue 27 Set! Hut!

Emmitt Smith broke the prestigious 1,000-yard rushing mark every season from 1991 to 2001.

The Cowboys made the playoffs three more times in the late '90s. But with each passing season, they became less of a championship threat. Coach Johnson was gone, and Aikman and Irvin both retired by 2001. Despite the efforts of such players as star offensive lineman Larry Allen, the Cowboys fell from the playoff picture in the first seasons of the new century. One steady presence in Dallas throughout these years was Emmitt Smith. In 2002, the longtime star gained his 16,727th career rushing yard to surpass Chicago Bears great Walter Payton as the NFL's all-time rushing leader.

After a 5–11 season in 2002, team owner Jerry Jones decided that a coaching change was needed once again. Jones then hired Bill Parcells, who had previously led the New York Giants to two Super Bowl victories, to build the Cowboys back into a champion. "There will be changes here," the stern and demanding coach promised. "No doubt about that."

Selected in the 2002 NFL Draft, receiver Antonio Bryant was one of the Cowboys' rising stars.

Bill Parcells rebuilt the 2003 Cowboys into a force ^

Linebacker Dat Nguyen was a tackling machine ^

Before the 2003 season, Dallas decided to re-lease Smith and rebuild with young players. And with Coach Parcells guiding such rising stars as quarterback Quincy Carter, wide receiver Antonio Bryant, hard-nosed safety Roy Williams, linebacker Dat Nguyen, and cornerback Terrence Newman, the Cowboys improved faster than anyone expected. By the end of the 2003 season, Dallas was 10–6 and back in the playoffs.

The Dallas Cowboys have a history of success that can be matched by few teams in the NFL. In a little more than four decades, the 'Boys have won five Super Bowls, appeared in 14 NFC champion-ship games, and featured some of the brightest stars in the history of pro football. As a new gen-eration of players now don the helmet with the lone star, "America's Team" hopes to soon become America's champs once again.

INDEX>